An **ama** Management Briefing

8

An ama Management Briefing

Idea Management:
How to Motivate
Creativity and Innovation

Charles H. Clark

ama
com A Division of
American Management Associations

Library of Congress Cataloging in Publication Data

Clark, Charles Hutchinson
   Idea management.

   (An AMA management briefing)
   1. Creative ability in business. 2. Employee
motivation. 3. Management. I. Title. II. Series:
American Management Associations. An AMA management
briefing.
HD53.C56   658.3'14   80-26870
ISBN 0-8144-2256-X

© 1980 AMACOM

A division of American Management Associations, New York.
All rights reserved. Printed in the United States of America.

This Management Briefing has been distributed to all members enrolled in the American Management Associations. A limited supply of extra copies is available at $5.00 a copy for AMA members, $7.50 a copy for nonmembers.

Third Printing

Preface

THE FIRST Chapter of *Idea Management* raises a question: Has Yankee ingenuity, like other of our precious resources, become a thing of the past? Mr. Clark, of course, doesn't believe it has, and neither do we. But we must agree with him when he says that the leading "innovation indicators" are pointing toward a "recession of creativity." The threat of that recession has prompted a number of American corporations to establish companywide innovation programs and to seek out other ways of revitalizing creativity.

An innovation program, as Mr. Clark points out, should show a great deal of ingenuity on the part of management. And it should reach all levels of the company. We realize, from the start, that not all ideas will prove valuable. But all employees have the potential to develop workable ideas that contribute to corporate goals. This is what Charles J. Pilliod, Jr., chairman of Goodyear, meant when he said, "Our ability to come up with new products, processes, and services is vital to maintain industry leadership. In the complexities of modern business, we need innovative thinking and results from all activities, whether it be in finance, industrial relations, manufacturing, purchasing, marketing, or whatever. Because we have a quality product or a good process doesn't mean it's the best we can do. The growing company of today has to be ready for change."

I feel fortunate to work in an environment where the need for change and the necessity for innovation are recognized.

Unlike other booklets, this one not only warns against the dangers of complacency but tells us ways to turn those "innovation indicators" around. In a sense, it's a self-help book. I am certain that others will benefit from reading it as much as I have.

John R. Hanlon
Chairman, Goodyear International
Innovation Policy Committee

Contents

About the Author

Charles H. Clark is founder and president of Yankee Ingenuity Programs, in Kent, Ohio, a firm offering workshops to stimulate creativity and innovation in industry, government, schools, and the voluntary sector. Prior to starting his own organization, he was senior education and training consultant at the BFGoodrich Institute for Personnel Development, headquartered at Kent State University. Earlier, he had been president of the Idea Laboratory, Pittsburgh, Pennsylvania, and director of the organization development program with the National Association of Manufacturers. As vice president of the Center for Independent Action, he developed an "idea corps" plan to help voluntary associations improve their programs and services.

In addition to his articles on management education techniques, Mr. Clark authored *Brainstorming* (Doubleday, 1958) as well as two privately copyrighted manuals on creativity, *How to Brainstorm for Profitable Ideas* (1966) and *The Crawford Slip Writing Method* (1978). Earlier, he had been an editorial assistant to Alex Osborn for *Applied Imagination*.

He has conducted workshops on creativity for such firms as Shell, Boeing, Standard Oil of California, IBM, Union Carbide, and General Mills, as well as for the United States Navy. Mr. Clark received his undergraduate degree from Harvard University in 1943 and a master's degree in education from the University of Pennsylvania in 1953. He serves as a colleague of the Buffalo Creative Education Foundation.

1

Introduction

"New England's most valuable natural resource weighs three pounds and wakes up at six in the morning. The Yankee brain."

SO read an advertisement from the First National Bank of Boston. Indeed, the value of that three-pound resource is recognized around the world. Among its products are the innovations, inventions, ingenious solutions—call them what you will—that have helped make the American dream.

That Yankee brain appears to be quite healthy. Recent innovations signal its vitality: laser technology, genetic engineering, cable television, microcircuitry, and photovoltaic solar cells, to name a few. But innovation is more than technological change, and inventiveness is not restricted to engineering and R&D. Inventiveness and innovation apply to everything we do—from selling to budgeting. Ninety percent of the cost of any new product comes after R&D. But talk about innovation rarely addresses *this* question: How can workers at every stage of bringing a product to the public contribute creatively to its development, manufacture, and marketing? By not asking the question, we tend to overlook our most valuable natural resource—the creative talents of our whole work force.

We plan to spend billions of dollars developing synthetic fuels and billions to clean up coal as an energy source. If we devoted a small fraction of those billions to establishing corporate environments in which employees were motivated—and freed—to spot opportunities and solve problems, and to improve the quality of their work lives, we would release creative energy comparable to the Manhattan Project's release of nuclear power.

Inflation, energy costs, reduced productivity, competition from the foreign sector—these are a few of the challenges of the 1980s. What we need, then, is a resurgence of inventiveness, not just in R&D, but in boardrooms and sales offices and shop floors.

AN INNOVATION RECESSION?

Occasionally, we hear talk that America has reached the end of a cycle. Indeed, 100 years have passed since Thomas Edison made light with a glass bulb. True, we seem to have depleted many of our natural resources. And productivity growth continues to slump toward zero. A June 4, 1979, Newsweek article carried the provoking title, "Innovation: Has America Lost its Edge?" That article quotes James G. Cook, president of the Thomas Edison Foundation, as saying, "Over the last decade, America has been losing its traditional leadership in innovation. Our Edison-like spirit of inventiveness seems to be going the way of the gas lamp."

The suggestion is that America is facing an innovation recession. There are, of course, no innovation indicators to rival our standard economic indicators. Measuring—and forecasting—innovation carries considerable risk. We could, perhaps, invent a set of indicators. Such items as the percent of gross national product budgeted for R&D, the number of new patents issued, and productivity trends, taken together, might signal the health of (and confidence in) American ingenuity.

Most of the innovation indicators have been pointing downward for some time—well in advance of the 1980 recession. The 1979 McGraw-Hill survey of business plans indicated that money allocated for R&D, taken as a percentage of GNP, had reached a 23-year low. The number of patents issued to Americans had declined to only 80 percent of its 1971 high.

Early warnings of an innovation recession have been on the horizon for several years. In 1978, the White House called for a sweeping, 28-agency review of the role of government in stimulating innovation. The recommendations that grew from that study will impact several areas. Some reform of the patent process has already been completed, with more to come. And the government is likely to raise its direct investment in new technology. Further, we may well see changes in federal tax policy to make it easier for manufacturers to acquire the equipment necessary to put a new product into production.

But no bureaucracy can hand out a quick cure for a lack of courage or provide a health plan for inventiveness. Nor can legislation create corporate environments that nurture innovation.

WHY AN INNOVATION RECESSION?

It's easy to blame "the government" for actions that have sapped innovative strength. Demands for no-risk, pollution-free products and processes have forced corporations to pump larger percentages of their capital budgets into investments in safety and pollution control. And there are other scapegoats: scarce money, an unfavorable tax structure, patent red tape, and antitrust laws that keep a corporation from capturing too large a share of one market. Why bother to innovate?

The goose that is ready to lay a golden egg may find herself tied up in patent delays and flogged by representatives from the Food and Drug Administration—and that gosling may never be hatched.

If you prefer, you can blame other factors: the depletion of inexpensive natural resources, the apparent decline in the number of high-quality engineering graduates, shortsighted corporate planning, and workers' demands for higher wages for less work.

Other causes of the innovation recession are more subtle. Regulation and uniformity have been manufactured into every phase of industrial life. True, these make possible low-cost products of unvarying quality. But we must pay a price. Organizations must stress conforming behavior if they are to keep products uniform. Now that we need flexibility and originality, we find them hard to come by.

Then, too, management has become a "science." Modern managers master skills for planning, organizing, and controlling. Administrative skills stabilize an organization. But effective administration, in turn, tends to snuff out deviations from set patterns. Following "the right way to do things around here" becomes more important than achieving results that matter.

But the most basic cause of our innovation recession is much simpler than any of these reasons. Simply put, we have yet to supply managers with the tools of creativity and the opportunity to use them. Any employee, given a piece of graph paper and five minutes of the right kind of explanation and encouragement, will list five or more ways to improve the effectiveness of his work by 20 percent. This has been demonstrated, over and over, in innovation seminars and other forms of creativity training.

So, heaping blame on the government, or on management training, or on anything else, wastes energy. In like manner, yakking at people to solve the company's problems, or to be more productive, or to be more innovative, accomplishes nothing. It's like handing an old-fashioned bamboo pole to a pole vaulter and prodding him to jump higher. For 15 years, the record for bamboo-pole vaulting peaked at 15 feet, 7 inches. With the introduction of the fiberglass pole, the record soared to 18 feet, 8 inches.

New tools make old problems easier to solve. The simplest of carpenter's tools—a screwdriver or a hammer—gives tremendous torque or impact. The simplest of creative tools adds to our idea power, our ability to twist and crack a tough problem. These tools work because they strengthen the way our minds naturally produce novel solutions. They give a partly conscious control over those invisible mental operations that have always been going on. We all respect the tremendous power of information processing tools to enhance our logical and analytical ability. The creative side our mind needs its own tools.

A creative environment begins with a few individuals who respect and support each other as "idea persons." They have some insight into creativity and a modest degree of success with the tools of creativity. Success ripples outward. Their efforts seed others.

Without that insight, support, and success, creativity is like any other management fad that has its day and fades. A splash in the company newspaper may stir up interest, and posters that say "Be Creative" may brighten up the halls. But such campaigns usually do little more than give employees the notion that they ought, somehow, to be doing things differently.

The next chapter offers some insights into the nature of creativity and the kind of environment that nurtures creative growth. The later chapters present the tools and techniques for building the environment.

2

The Company Environment: An Idea Plant

CERTAIN professionals—artists and musicians, for example—have cultural permission to be eccentric. We tolerate, even support, their nonconformity until eccentricity, unfortunately, becomes synonymous with creativity. Nothing could be further from the truth. Creativity has very little to do with deviations in dress or affectations in behavior.

The word "creativity" in itself can make some persons uncomfortable. We think about creative art, creative music, creative writing, but rarely about creative business. Often, words like "ingenuity" or "resourcefulness" make us more comfortable. But there's nothing wrong with "creativity," as long as we have a clear picture of what we're talking about.

UNDERSTANDING CREATIVITY

Shortly after World War II, the United States Navy supported Dr. J. P. Guilford's research into the dimensions of creative behavior. These studies, conducted at the University of Southern California, established the cornerstone for much of our present-day understanding of the subject. Dr. Guilford's most important breakthrough came in the identification of five key creative elements: fluency, flexibility, originality, awareness, and drive. His analysis removes part of the mystery. It allows us to think about creativity more comprehensively.

Our ability to be deliberately creative grows with our understanding of the process. Let's look at Dr. Guilford's elements more carefully.

Dissecting Creativity

Fluency. The word is used here in the sense of "fluent speech." Ideas pour out of our heads like a waterfall. We measure fluency by quantity—the total number of ideas in a set period. For example: "How many round objects can you name in four minutes?" "How many uses can you think of for a paper clip?" "How many different ways can you use baking soda?" For a four-minute period, the average number of responses on a simple question like, "How many round objects. . .?" runs around 22. The range is from 8 to 32.

Flexibility. Fluency and flexibility come from a person's ability to let go of categories. Given permission, the mind sails a zigzag course of free association through memory, sense impressions, and an imagined future. Flexibility indicates nimbleness in hopping from one category to another. It is measured in terms of the total number of categories represented in a stream of ideas.

For example, in naming round objects, the output might skip from street lamps and car lights to push-button switches and then to buttons, eyelets, and armholes. The leap from one category to another—from lights to switches to clothing—demonstrates flexibility.

Without being aware of it, most persons automatically exhaust one category before moving on to another. Others list one or two related objects before moving to the next classification. Creativity exercises increase the number and variety in both kinds of people.

Originality. Out of 500 respondents listing round objects, most persons in the creativity seminars mention common items—coins or balls. Fewer write down the hole in a donut, manhole covers, or gears. These responses are statistically uncommon. We call this unusualness "originality." Originality for different populations can be measured: the fewer times an idea appears, the greater its originality.

Awareness. This refers to the ability to see with our minds and imaginations as well as with our eyes. Some people look at a small seed as a yellow grain of corn. Others look at the same speck and see a stalk with ears of corn that can produce a whole garden of grain. Awareness means seeing the interconnections that form the meaning of the larger picture.

Most people looked at an empty New Jersey bowling alley as just a bowling alley. One grocery store owner saw it as the space large enough for the superstore he wanted to build, with triple the stock of the stores around him. He could turn it back into a bowling alley if his idea flopped. His awareness paid off. Customers thronged to his huge store. He was a pioneer in what became one of the dominant food-store chains in the Middle Atlantic states.

Drive. By drive we mean motivation, the willingness to try and try again. Drive multiplies the effectiveness of each of the other elements. With fluency, it means the willingness to think up another bucket of ideas if the first ones don't work. With flexibility, it means coming at the problem from still another angle.

The commitment to solve a problem creatively is not at all like the commitment to a straitjacket. Nor does drive mean the steel-jawed, do-or-die efforts of a workaholic. Creative drive means trying a variety of doors until one leads to the path to one's goal. It doesn't mean frantic pounding on one door and bewailing one's fate because that door won't open.

Creating Creativity

A new idea "happens" when someone discovers a new combination, arrangement, or adaptation of existing ideas. Things, people, or ideas become connected as no one has connected them before. The connection may already exist in nature, and the "new idea" is only a matter of seeing a pattern for the first time.

Thus, Pasteur noted a relationship between microbes and spoiled wine. He later noted a connection between different microbes and the anthrax that was killing sheep. Once he discovered the pattern, others saw new applications. Later, a Glasgow surgeon made the connection that microbes in the air were causing putrefaction and death after surgery. He blessed all mankind by developing aseptic surgery.

The same discovery of links and adaptations characterizes smaller "Ahas!"—the kind you and I get. Thus, a San Francisco advertising salesman combined sample restaurant menus into a bound booklet to be sold, by the thousands, to tourists.

At times, the simplest adaptation can supply the missing link. In 1890, the United States Department of the Census first used tab cards to store and process information. But a problem developed that plagued the industry and tab-card users for 75 years. Cards bent as they were processed. They jammed the machinery. One would think that somebody in the manufacturer's organizations or in the thousands of users in government agencies, banks, railroads, and other companies would come up with a solution. People lived with the problem until an IBM engineer at Greencastle, Indiana, where most cards are printed, came up with the solution. *Round the corners.*

Why does it take 75 years to come up with such a simple solution? That question is probably unanswerable. We do know, however, that greater fluency, flexibility, originality, awareness, and drive increases the probability that a person will see a new combination of adaptation. A person can stimulate himself or herself to see links, connections, and recombinations by posing questions such as those found in the S-C-A-M-P-E-R checklist, page 16.

Creativity and Logic

Persons who make a living from their imaginations show a distaste for logical methodologies. In similar fashion, those who take pride in their logical thinking turn up their noses at the randomness of free-association techniques. A leading book illustrator and designer put it this way: "Logic is good for one thing: postmortems. That's how you find out why something didn't work. Creativity is different. It's like stepping onto new but somehow familiar ground. And you feel in your bones that what you're going to do is *right*. Even though you can't prove it to someone else."

Step-by-step methods of problem solving are often part of management training. Tens of thousands of executives and managers in 53 countries have taken the Kepner-Tregoe course on problem solving and decision making. The course provides an organized method for troubleshooting. Something has gone wrong, and someone must diagnose the problem, root out the cause, and fix things up. Kepner-Tregoe analytical tools are amazingly effective in making correct diagnoses. And creativity techniques help generate alternative ways to handle the causes of the problem, once they are found.

We've all heard other teachers drone on and on about defining a problem carefully, gathering facts, and projecting costs and benefits of alternative solutions before reaching a decision. Hundreds of books have been written on this approach. But few persons—not even those who teach it—follow the method in real life. Our minds hop, skip, and jump. Solutions zoom in before all the steps are taken. Everyone has had the experience of being unable to untie a knotty problem. We may be doing something

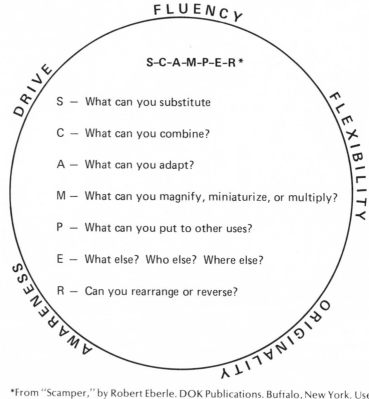

FLUENCY

S-C-A-M-P-E-R*

S — What can you substitute

C — What can you combine?

A — What can you adapt?

M — What can you magnify, miniaturize, or multiply?

P — What can you put to other uses?

E — What else? Who else? Where else?

R — Can you rearrange or reverse?

DRIVE

FLEXIBILITY

AWARENESS

ORIGINALITY

*From "Scamper," by Robert Eberle. DOK Publications. Buffalo, New York. Used with permission.

16

else—not thinking about the problem at all. Then, all of a sudden an idea flashes into the mind, and the whole knot unravels.

Oscillating between the creative and the step-by-step method is best. Logic is made up of an orderly attack—on A, then B, then C. The creative process zigzags, then leaps into a new category—from C to P without going through the steps in between. One approach strengthens the other. What the artist quoted earlier didn't say (and probably wouldn't admit) is that analyses of past successes and failures provided an unconscious radar to the new ground.

Creativity and logical analysis may be hemispheres apart. But successful efforts often depend on the right sequence and combination of creative and analytical tools. Logical workmanship gives stability. But creative work prys open new possibilities.

Creativity frequently works in sudden hunches or insights. A new combination or adaptation scampers into awareness.

AN IDEA PLANT

Often someone at a meeting gets a little idea or hunch that he thinks will move the group toward a solution. As soon as the idea is brought into the open, someone will challenge it: "Why do you say that?" The person with the hunch is embarrassed because he can't immediately come up with five reasons why it's a good idea. Such supporting thoughts usually come later.

The same thing happens in other corners of the company—in conversations among workers or between a supervisor and the subordinates. A person who works at a job for eight hours a day gets that job into his system. He carries it with him, even when he's not consciously thinking about it. He has hunches about how things could be done a little differently to make things easier or more satisfying for himself or others. Those insights don't come from formal education or from a lot of reading; they come from doing the job.

But new ideas are fragile. They're tiny, unimportant-looking things, like seeds. The person who speaks up about his ideas feels a bit fragile, too. He knows that he has just opened himself up for criticism. And he will probably be the first person to admit that an idea sounds only partly baked.

Building the kind of company environment that supports innovation requires a cooperative—and conscious—suspension of judgment. People need to hold back those swift chops of logic that kill seeds before they take root. It also means developing "peripheral vision"—the opposite of tunnel vision. People need to be encouraged to look at the full implications of events: How does A affect R, S, and T—in addition to the obvious impact on B and C. It means setting up idea traps: some device for catching and holding the seeds until they can be evaluated and planted. Finally, it means giving employees both permission and encouragement for being creative. Let's take a look at each part of the creative environment.

Suspending Judgment

Consider the story of how the zipper came to replace buttons on men's trousers. The story goes back to the Hookless Fastener Company, now Talon, in the town of Meadville, Pennsylvania. A novice advertising salesman for the old *Saturday Evening Post* stopped in one day to solicit advertising. A Hookless Fastener executive confided in him. "Ninety percent of our zippers go into tobacco pouches. If anything happens to that business, we're out of luck."

The salesman asked where they were selling the other 10 percent. "BFGoodrich is trying some out on footwear and galoshes," was the reply, "and a women's clothing manufacturer is starting to put some on clothes."

The salesman reflected for a moment. "Why not sell them to men's clothing manufacturers to put on men's flies—instead of buttons?"

The idea went to the president of the company, whose judgment was incisive. "I like trousers the way they are. Buttons are safer. We could get into trouble; we might have lawsuits."

It took the company four years to produce the first experimental pair of zipper-fly trousers.

Any organization has a stock of about 100 negative phrases like, "That idea could get us into trouble." They are referred to as "killer phrases," and their power as idea stoppers permeates industry. People don't relish being put down by sarcasm and ridicule: "You call *that* an idea?" Nor do they enjoy being misunderstood: "We're doing that already." Nor do they welcome being put in their places: "You know, we *pay* experts to think about things like that." People want to protect their feelings, so they clam up.

Most killer phrases are self-protective for the person who says them. They shelter the speaker's ego, or protect personal territory or provide that sense of security that comes from following established procedures. Rule 816 has earned its place beside Murphy's Law and the Peter Principle.

Rule 816: Relating to New Ideas

Rule 816 is now in effect until further notice. When confronted with a new idea, vote against it.

Rationale:
1. It is probably not a good idea; new ideas seldom are.
2. Even if it is a good idea, the chances are it will never be tested.
3. Even if it is a good idea and even though it is tested, chances are that it won't work the first time.
4. Even if it is a good idea, and even though it is tested, and even if it succeeds, there'll be plenty of time for thinking up alibis.

Therefore:
When confronted with a new idea, the rational action is to take a positive and forward-looking stand against it.

Allowed to mature, killer phrases get elaborated into position papers and reports. Consider the 1861 congressional debate over the appropriation of funds to establish the Smithsonian Institution. One senator is on record as stating, "What do we care about stuffed snakes, alligators, and all such things. . . here is an appropriation of $6,000 for the most worthless purpose." *The Congressional Globe* includes these comments on the purchase of Alaska, again by a senator: "The possession of this Russian territory can give us neither honor, wealth, nor power, but will always be a source of weakness and expense without any adequate return." Even a creative genius can falter, as when Thomas Edison wrote, "My personal desire would be to prohibit entirely the use of alternating currents. They are as unnecessary as they are dangerous."

You can't get hot water out of a spigot while the cold water is on. All you can get is lukewarm water. The same is true for information. We can't get hot ideas out of people's heads while the cold water of criticism is turned on. At best, we get lukewarm ideas. The creative mind works through free association. We let ideas flow out in this illogical fashion. Later, we can put them through the sieve of judgment to screen out those that seem valuable for the purpose at hand.

Alex Osborn started brainstorming as a technique for solving advertising and marketing problems. He saw how killer phrases kept popping up during creative sessions, and he wondered what would happen if he forbade these phrases completely during brainstorming. To his happy surprise, forbidding criticism and judgment increased creative productivity.

Any deliberate creative effort requires a conscious suspension of judgment. And building a corporate environment that nourishes innovation starts with an across-the-board agreement to suspend judgment in the presence of new ideas. A campaign to label and exterminate the killer phrases clears the air. All personnel need to be warned about the unconscious use of rule 816—that tendency to ride with the safety of the status quo, or modest change at best.

Peripheral Vision and Flexibility

The top management of a supermarket chain with 106 stores felt that their store managers were blind to the problems in their own stores. They noticed that managers could walk down their own aisles a hundred times without seeing anything wrong. In another person's store, they could spot all the faults.

The company developed an ingenious two-part solution. First, they scheduled each manager to visit another manager's store once a month and list the things that needed correction. Secondly, the company sent each manager out to shop at a competitor's supermarket once a month. Attention was directed to what the other stores were doing right, and the managers were challenged to adapt those ideas to their own stores.

The longer a person works in the same routine with the same people, the more he becomes a victim of "job blindness" or "tunnel vision."

Killer Phrases

"You're on the wrong track."

"Not enough return on investment."

"Let's shelve that idea for awhile."

"Who is going to do it?"

"What do you know about it?"

"I don't understand what you hope to accomplish."

"How does that concern you?"

"So what else is new?"

"The boss will laugh."

"We tried that two years ago."

"Competition has taken the lead."

"It's great—but. . ."

"Who asked you?"

"We're too big for that."

"The public is not ready yet."

"It won't fit our operation."

"The sixth floor won't like it."

"It won't hold water."

"It's too risky."

"We already have too much to worry about."

"You're too young to know anything about that."

"Someone must have done it."

"Be sensible."

"I thought of that last year, we didn't use it then."

"You've got to be kidding."

"Who needs it?"

"That's against all of our combined logic."

"What for?"

"Why not start today?"

"Who can't afford that?"

"You'll never get approval."

"We tried that 25 years ago."

"It's not a new concept."

"I can't sell it."

"It's probably illegal."

"The public will laugh at us."

"Let's check on it later."

"We've got enough problems already."

"Why?"

"Someday there may be a need for this."

"What are you? Some kind of nut?"

"Why do that now?"

Rigidity and uniformity are built into every aspect of industry. We demand that every article coming off the production line be identical with every other article. We want one can of tomato soup to taste like every other can of that brand's tomato soup. And a person needs to know that he is expected to be at a certain work station at a certain time and that a paycheck is coming next Friday. As a result, habitual actions produce convergent thoughts.

Innovation calls for "kinkyformity": a respect for proven ways of doing things, but the flexibility to see a broader picture.

Take, for example, the principles of management by objective and management by exception, both valuable concepts of modern management. Used repeatedly and without sensitivity to a broader picture, they narrow the manager's vision to predictable results and negative deviations. Much energy is expended on figuring out why things go wrong. Little attention is placed on figuring out why things went well—or better than expected.

Think about the story of the Prince Castle Malted Mixer. This appliance made six milk shakes at the same time. Ray Kroc, then their sales representative, sensed an unusual positive deviation when a San Bernadino foodstand ordered eight machines, enough to mix 48 shakes at the same time. His curiosity aroused, Kroc flew from Chicago to California to see why someone needed eight of his mixers for one location. This brought about the connection of Mr. Kroc and the McDonald brothers. Each of the next 16 million shakes that followed was a product of his curiosity about that positive deviation.

After hearing the milk shake story, one manager commented: "We never look at things in just that way. We put all our attention on the stores that don't meet their targets. We have others that never give us any trouble—they're always above goal. It never occurred to me to find out what they are doing to cause these positive deviations. Maybe we'd find some difference about them that we could adapt in our other stores."

The opposite of management by exception is management by positive deviation. One principle in no way invalidates the other. And there's no reason why a manager can't be flexible enough to use both. Skill in problem solving is vital to success, but skill in opportunity finding makes men and organizations the real winners.

It's easy to slip into a mental rut. A creative viewpoint is not so much a "breakthrough" as a "breakout." A person bursts into new territory by going beyond those first, easy-to-come-by thoughts. It's as if one has to purge his mind of the ordinary ideas before breaking out and discovering the fresh territory. It takes peripheral vision to spot what's coming in from the sidelines. And it takes flexibility to step up into the stands—or go to the other end of the field—to view things from a different angle.

How can a company make peripheral vision part of its innovative environment? Most commonly, this is done by bringing in a consultant—an outsider who can view an operation or problem from a fresh perspective. But there are plenty of ways for doing it within the company—simply by giving people an opportunity to step back from their desks or work stations and view an entire operation. Once broad areas of opportunity are defined, personnel from one department can view operations in another department, or another plant, as part of an idea campaign. This cross-fertilization, handled in a supportive and nonthreatening manner, can pay off in new insights. Also, the techniques for group creativity—discussed in Chapter 4—can knock holes in tunnel vision.

Idea Traps

It's too easy for higher levels of management to forget that the persons working down there on the shop floor, or in the receiving room, or on the loading dock are the real experts on their parts of the business. Each person has ideas galore on how to make the work easier or tie in better with other parts of the company. They know their jobs better than the persons who send them the materials to work on or the paperwork to process. They know little about the president's job or the vice president's, because that work is outside their realm of experience. But each person is an expert on his or her own job.

The customer service department of a large office machine firm faced an embarrassingly high error rate in dispatching customer engineers. Calls for service came through a switchboard, where an operator took down the relevant information. Data on location, type of machine, territory, and customer engineer were number-coded on a card, and the card was sent on a conveyor belt to the radio dispatcher. It was unthinkable, of course, for a leader in the information processing field to get the number codes mixed up, but that was exactly what happened. A dispatcher in the Chicago office came up with the solution: give each customer cards with the correct number codes for their machines. Have the customer read off those codes when calling for service.

For years, BFGoodrich sent out packages of tire owners' warranties by parcel post—always 50 in a pacakage. Fees varied from 66 cents to $2.35 each, depending on the distance. Someone asked, "Why do we have to send 50 in a pacakage?" There was no reason. Removing four warranties from each package brought the weight down to less than a pound. Now the postage was only 66 cents, regardless of distance. And the hours spent zoning and pricing each parcel were no longer necessary.

An idea trap is any system for catching ideas. Executives management can use considerable ingenuity in establishing the trap lines. They can be as complex as periodic "take the idea to the top" campaigns or ongoing programs of incentive awards for cost-saving innovations. They can be as simple as a series of idea sessions in each department, using the tools for creativity given in this briefing.

Each worker should be considered the expert on his or her segment of the business. So the idea traps should be broad enough to draw from all personnel. Not all ideas, of course, will prove valuable. But if only one workable idea could be mined from each employee, any corporation would be running miles ahead of its competitors.

Motivation

What motivates people to give their ideas to a company? Certainly, incentive awards, badges, advancement opportunities, and recognition in the company newspaper all add up. Management can be as creative as it likes about providing incentives. Something as simple as a month's parking place next to the vice president's— right up front, near the entrance—has proved effective at one company.

Incentives are effective motivators, but pride, self-respect, and

24

doing something worthwhile are even more compelling. The phenomenal success of Japanese quality circles (QCs) is a case in point.

Trained in analytical as well as creative problem solving, the quality circles (usually eight to 12 workers) meet on company time to deal with safety, quality control, and production problems in their area. Early in 1980, the quality circle movement attracted a great deal of attention in America. At first, the topic attracted a swarm of killer phrases: "Just try it and see what the union does!" "Fine—if your workers are all dedicated professionals."

Except that the idea does work—as Westinghouse, RCA, Lockheed, and over 100 other American corporations are finding out.

In 1979, the Technology Transfer Institute dispatched a team of American industrial managers to explore the state of the art in quality control in Japan. The study mission returned with new insights on how the Japanese achieved their astonishing reputation for quality products in the short period since World War II.

The quality circle idea fits Japanese society: a common language and cultural heritage, and a uniformly high degree of education. Labor unions are established vertically, one union per corporation. The concept of "lifetime" employment, along with a corporate commitment to no lay-offs, establishes a high degree of job security.

But worker pride in the workplace and management's expectation of innovative participation are at the root of quality circle success. That workers are taught to think creatively builds self-esteem. To ensure quality, the QC is often given a major responsibility in training new workers. In many corporations, the quality circle has a target for submitting a specified number of recommendations each year. Management is then required to implement a specified percentage of those recommendations.

One member of the study mission reported a ritualistic litany, recited with sincere commitment by host representatives from almost every corporation visited. The speech went something like this:

Japan's population of 115 million . . . half that of the United States, lives in a country not much bigger than the state of Montana. The land has virtually no resources, and only 15 percent of it is arable. . . . By necessity, Japan's role has to be that

25

of importer of low-value resources and exporter of high value-added manufactured products. To assure fulfillment of this role, Japanese goods must be regarded as offering high quality at competitive cost in all trading countries.[1]

The study-mission participant concluded that QCs were only part of the picture. A management commitment to excellence, based on hard facts of geography and economics, cascaded down to all levels of the organization. This commitment was the prime mover. Japan had to be "just a little bit better" if it was to survive.

A clearly communicated, socially important goal ripples outward to all parts of the industrial enterprise. Workers see the connection of their jobs to a national destiny. Each Japanese company has its own motto, which translates the national survival code into positive, product-related terms. For example, each can of paint at Kansai helps mankind by "Making Lives Richer and More Colorful."

Finally, then, workers share their ideas for the same reasons that persons do woodworking or design their own homes. They want to take pride in seeing something of themselves "out there," put into tangible form that matters. The worker can say, "My ideas help build my company. I make a difference; I count."

[1]John F. McAllister, "The Quality/Culture Interrelationship," presentation at the American Management Associations seminar, "Using Japanese Quality Control and Productivity Techniques in U.S. Industry," New York, April 24, 1980.

3

Tools for Working
with Your Own Ideas

A CREATIVE viewpoint is a fresh way of looking at things. A person starts to see ideas everywhere, in objects, in people, and in events.

Think of it this way: we live in an idea museum. There's the paint on the wall, the light switch, the paper clips in the desk drawer, the discarded envelope in the wastebasket. When we trace it back far enough, every object started in the mind of one person. Someone had an idea; someone acted on it.

A person can be in any part of his idea museum—a taxi, an airplane, a doctor's waiting room—and ask, "I wonder where *this* object came from." Certainly, most of the objects on display were helped along by some industrial process. But the most sophisticated R&D department together with the most intelligent planning, decision making, forecasting, and marketing can't amount to much until someone comes up with a good idea to trigger the rest.

Rummaging through the idea museum puts us in direct contact with the history of inventiveness. These are the ideas that worked—as their very inclusion in the museum indicates. It is encouraging to realize that the biggest ideas started in humble ways.

This curiosity prompts a continual questioning: "How was this thing made?" "Who had this idea first?" "Why is it shaped like this?" Often, one finds himself reading encyclopedia or journal articles to find the answers. For some, it means visiting a library at least once a month—skimming the shelves, dipping into magazines that seem unrelated to professional responsibilities. There's exciting material there, especially in the foreign publications.

The more ideas one sees, the greater the likelihood that a new combination or extension will occur. The subconscious mind is always moving. Ideas surface at bizarre times: when we shower, play tennis, or rake the yard. No one needs to read Freud to use the subconscious. Often, a simple willingness to welcome the unexpected discovery does the trick.

For Bill N. Smith, an engineer with BFGoodrich, the solution for preventing brake drag on the Boeing 727 landing wheels came when his wife asked him to sweep the front porch. He noticed the washer-type locking device used to keep the screen door open. Curiosity about how the gadget worked opened up the solution he was looking for.

The idea for Bisquick (which set the pattern for all the baking mixes that followed) came in 1933 when a sales executive for a subsidiary of General Mills was riding late at night on the Southern Pacific Railroad. Delighted to find freshly baked biscuits still served in the dining car at that hour, he asked the chef how the miracle had been performed. The chef explained the process of premixing he had come up with. The sales executive turned the idea over to General Mills' head chemist for development. It took considerable ingenuity to come up with the formula that gave proper shelf life, but the efforts paid off.

The creative viewpoint starts with a willingness to see ideas everywhere. Other techniques and tools help.

WRITING IT DOWN

Many people handle their ideas carelessly. Faced with a new insight, a person thinks, "I'll have to remember that and do something about it when I get back to the office." But the office has its own demands—phone calls to be answered and appointments to be rearranged. The seed gets lost.

A record-keeping system and a monthly review of the random ideas leads to an astonishing discovery of how active the mind is.

The record-keeping system need not be elaborate. At all times, carry a notepad or pack of index cards. Then, set up an idea bank: a box on the desk, hall table, or bureau. Do not attempt to evaluate or implement an idea when it pops into your mind. Write it down and deposit it in the idea bank. Periodically, read through the slips and sort them into categories. This acts as a kind of reseeding that creates a context for more ideas to pop up—again at unexpected moments.

The habit of writing things down seems too simple to mention. But how many people do it? Occasionally, someone takes out a notepad in the middle of a meeting and begins writing frantically. A speaker's random remark—something that might have seemed trivial to the rest of the audience—set his or her mind spinning with significant associations.

THINKING UP

Suspending judgment applies as much to personal living as to working. No doubt everyone has a cadre of private killer phrases to suffocate his or her inventiveness. "I'll never find time for that." "What will the neighbors think?" "I'll never get the money to do it."

Note how the killer phrases protect against failure. Rationalizing why something won't work provides the strongest excuse for not putting time and effort into it.

A written inventory of private idea stoppers brings them into the open. Once exposed, they can be manipulated. Also, suspending judgment on one's own ideas helps a person be more open to ideas from others. A reputation for curiosity and open-mindedness attracts those who need to share their thoughts. This sets up a win/win climate for creative achievement, rather than the poisonous win/lose or lose/lose climate of, "I guess I'm not supposed to do any thinking around here. I'll just do what I'm told."

Unfortunately, much of our formal education teaches us to be critics. The student who rips a thesis apart or criticizes a theory is rewarded with higher grades. Thinking down is easy. Thinking up alternatives is much harder. As one manager put it, "Be sure to ask 'what's good about it?' before grumbling about what's bad."

Within the last several decades, problem-solving approaches became fashionable in our universities. Courses such as "Problems in History," "Problems in Sociology," and "Problems in Economics" entered the curriculum. The problem-solving orientation may well prod students into thinking through issues, but it also educates them to view the world as a string of problems. Seldom is there a course in opportunity finding.

Yet, opportunities encircle us. Here, an understanding of what one does best becomes the best tool for gripping an opportunity. Many career/life planning programs begin with concentrated, and very positive, self-assessment: long lists of skills, values, and accomplishments. These are the assets and positive deviations of personal living.

An idea from the idea bank, matched with a sense of personal assets and an understanding of positive deviations, helps a person seize an opportunity.

USING THE IMAGINATION

Look at how easily a child slips into imagining. A tree stump becomes a car or airplane. An old blanket becomes a tent, or a discarded piece of adult clothing becomes an excuse for role-playing and make-believe.

We live in two worlds. There is the world of reality: projects, deadlines, and budgets. The other is the world of imagination: making changes, improvements, doing things differently. We should take a few steps upward into the world of imagination, grab an idea, and engineer some link between that concept and the real world. We must *make* it work; reduce it to practice. There's no reason to be afraid of wild ideas. Those ideas need to be captured, tamed, and made part of our domestic life.

If we lacked imagination, the human race would be living in caves and repeating what our ancestors did thousands of years ago. Birds still build their nests the way their ancestors did in the past. All animals except man must repeat themselves over and over. In endowing us with imagination, our Creator made our man-made civilization possible. For the first time in history, we are seriously studying how to enhance these creative powers. This is providential, because surely today we must "think or sink."

Try this experiment.

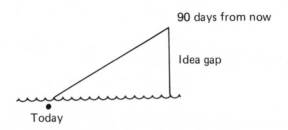

Imagine that the wavy line represents the way things are going now. Let the diagonal line represent what could be done differently 90 days from now. Take out a memo pad, slip of paper, or note cards. Relax as completely as possible. Now, focus on a question, such as:

How can I improve the quality of my family life?
How can we have the best vacation—or Christmas—ever?
How can I make my on-the-job performance more effective?

Suspend all negative response, such as, "I've tried that already" or "I'll never find the time for that." Let your imagination loose, as a child does when playing. Write down ideas as they come—wild ones as well as the commonplace. Write each idea on a separate slip of paper. Stop at the end of five minutes.

Done as a seminar activity, the average output per person is ten ideas for a five minute period. See if you can beat that average.

After a short break, return to the cards, sort them into categories, and use them to trigger more ideas. Again, limit the idea session to five minutes.

Deposit the ideas in the idea bank and let the matter rest. A week or so later, identify the most promising idea or combination of ideas. Repeat the exercise with the question of, "How can I implement this?"

RESPECTING INTUITIONS

We allow hunches and intuitions to enter our recreation, but tend to shove them aside when things get serious. In fact, words like "intuition" and "instinct" breed suspicion. But what else is it that tells the experienced fisherman to use a certain lure on a particular day, or the tennis player that his opponent is going to return the ball to a certain spot on the court.

Intuitions come from our subconscious minds. They have a certain feeling, like the artist's sense of moving to "new, but familiar ground."

Intense work with fact-finding and analysis sets the stage for the sudden hunch that comes later when mowing the lawn or fishing. Often, a creative person will go through a long period of studying an issue from all possible angles. Often, it appears that too much time is being expended on analysis. There won't be any time left for action. When the "Aha!" finally does pop to mind, it will be more effective, more elegant, simply because of the hours of slow cooking that preceded it.

This is usually the only way we can get ideas to solve the toughest problems. Such a process can be identified, studied, and learned, so that a person can depend on it when it's needed.

Forecasting, for example, always involves some degree of uncertainty. This is true no matter how carefully one has evaluated past performances, identified trends, and defined indicators. The final course of action should *look right*, based on the data available, and *feel right*, because of the grasp of the ways things work. Intuition should never be confused with impulsive or irresponsible guesswork.

MOVING OUT OF RUTS

Unthinking, habital behavior is ingenuity's worst enemy. Everyone gets into ruts without realizing it: the coffee break comes at the same time every morning; day after day the same forms are used for letters or for answering the phone. Before long, approaches to people, problems, and opportunities become predictable. The mystery, the sense of discovery, and the awareness that a person had when the job was "new" give way to safe routines.

Variety spurs ingenuity—new hobbies, different forms of recreation, simple rearrangements of home or office furniture, lunch with different persons from the office, a new route to the train station. Playtime with puzzles and challenging games activates the mind. Intense exercise jogs out the cobwebs.

Feeling one's way into someone else's point of view sometimes pulls a person out of a rut. Start with a member of the family—a child or your spouse. Imagine what it is like for that person to wake up in the morning. Picture his or her first sense impressions, responses to objects in the room, reactions to persons and things during the morning ritual. See the responsibilities he or she faces in the hours ahead. Which objects or events will bring joy? Which will evoke dread or guilt? If possible, actually hold one of the objects and examine it from the other person's point of view. Seeing with a child's eyes is especially challenging, but it often brings startling new perceptions.

Sometimes an imaginative step outside of one's cultural boundaries helps. As you approach a problem, ask how an American Indian would deal with the same situation. Put yourself in the place of an ancient Egyptian or Greek, or use any contemporary culture with which you have some familiarity. Or imagine that the objects associated with a particular problem were 100 times larger than in real life. How would the change in size necessitate a change in tools? What would happen if these objects were microscopic?

Stress can be creative: face the conflict or problem that's been simmering on the back burner for months. Call for an open confrontation, a sharing of frustrations, and an honest exchange of view. The confrontation may bring a fresh perspective for all persons involved.

Practice spontaneity. Many Americans lack a healthy sense of street dancing, that is, a chance to sing (no matter how poorly), dance, clap hands, and get in touch with everyone in the neighborhood, children and senior citizens alike. Since we have few national customs to enforce spontaneity, each person needs to develop his or her own forms.

EXERCISING THE CREATIVE CAPACITY

The creative muscle needs to be flexed and toned. Anyone can set up a personal "fitness" program based on the dimensions of creativity discussed in the previous chapter. How many uses for a paper clip *can* you think of in four minutes? Let the list grow, adding new uses that pop to mind hours later. Force yourself away from the common applications. An unbent paper clip, by the way, can be used as a coat hook, a spear for picking up an olive, or as an emergency replacement for a lost cufflink. Share the exercise with members of the family. Give applause or other recognition for originality. Extend the exercise to other objects: a brick, a coffee cup, or car tires.

Learn to recognize creativity in yourself and others. Starting with a member of your family or a close friend, ask the person to tell you about a creative idea, how he or she got it, and what it meant, finally, to others. Start a clipping file of creative ideas and innovative solutions, using stories, news articles, and advertisements you run across in your reading.

THE CREATIVE GROOVE

Imagine all the habits of creativity working together: continuous questioning about displays in the idea museum, the habits of writing things down and thinking up, exercising the imagination and the creative capacity, training the intuition, and prodding oneself out of ruts. The creative viewpoint is a very healthy and active state of mind. Certainly, ideas *are* everywhere—in people, objects, and events.

Creative persons have always been drawn together, both because of a shared respect for each other and because each needs to rub ideas against the other. The tools for group creativity, discussed in the next chapter, can be used alone, with a partner, at home with the family, at the club, or with a church group. As with any tool, skill develops with use.

4

Tools for Working
with Ideas as a Team

CRAWFORD SLIP WRITING

Why do most groups appear so uninventive? The answer, quite simply, is that no one has ever handed them an "idea tool kit" and shown them how to use the tools to better their lives and work.[2]

Most of the carpenter's tools we use are quite simple. Consider the design of a screwdriver: a single shaft with a handle and a dull blade. Nor is there anything very complex about a saw, hammer, or crowbar.

Crawford slip writing has the same simplicity. It can be used to collect dozens, even hundreds of ideas from any meeting, conference, or convention in just ten minutes. Even the shyest person expresses thoughts without fear of ridicule. No one knows who fathers each idea. Thus, it sidesteps the competition that happens when some members of a group try to outshine others. It produces a stockpile of ideas in a form that allows fast sorting into categories for action planning.

The method is simply this. Everyone at a meeting receives a pad of three-by-five inch slips of paper. The leader presents a problem

[2]Material in this chapter is based on *The Crawford Slip Writing Method* (1978) and *How to Brainstorm for Profitable Ideas* (1966) by Charles H. Clark.

statement in "how to" form. For example, "How can the Fullerton Chamber of Commerce improve its services to members?" The leader then explains the importance of holding back judgments and asks that each person write down as many answers to the question as the time period will allow. Each answer must be written on a separate slip.

The effectiveness of the method has been demonstrated at large conventions, with management teams, with professional societies, Rotary clubs, and other groups. Imagine a Sunday morning worship service in which the collection plates are passed twice—once for gifts of money, once for gifts of ideas.

The method is named after Professor C.C. Crawford, who invented it at the University of Southern California as one step in preparing training manuals. Beginners listed their difficulties with a certain operation in "how to" form. He then assembled panels of experts to write slips in answer to the beginner's difficulties.

Perhaps there is nothing terribly new in the concept. Dmitri Mendeleev, the Russian chemist who first outlined the pattern of atomic weights and chemical properties that led to the periodic table of elements, developed the habit of putting the name and properties of each known element on a separate card. His passion for solitaire led him to arrange and rearrange the cards. Working with incomplete and often inaccurate data, he discovered the structure on which all modern chemistry is based. Dmitri Mendeleev was, perhaps, the first slip writer in recorded history.

This description of slip writing provokes two questions:

- Why in the world does something so simple have so much power?
- How can I, as a manager, make the technique work for me?

Each question needs to be answered. Understanding how to use it comes from understanding why it works.

Why Slip Writing Works

Consider this story from a business forms company. Convinced that customer satisfaction (and increased repeat sales) depended on some form of consumer education, the marketing executive initiated a customer training program to teach people how to use the forms correctly. The program died. Reason: lack of support from the sales staff. He tried again several years later. Again it bombed.

The executive, after hearing about slip writing, invited each of his 11 sales districts to send a representative to a three-day conference at company headquarters. The first day, he used slip writing to get answers to the question, "How can we put together a purchaser training plan that can be counted on to retain salesmen's interests over an extended period?"

The slips were sorted into groups. The second and third days of the workshop were spent in refining ideas, using additional slip writing to elaborate on basic suggestions. Implemented eight weeks later, the finished plan produced a 50 percent surge in sales volume.

Several factors contributed to this success. In this firm, slip writing challenged everyone to become part of a team effort, rather than shine as individual idea persons. In addition, it made use of the company's real experts on salesmen's responses and customer behavior. The method also provided an oscillation between individual and group creativity—slip writing, followed by discussion groups, then more slip writing, along with judicial thinking in sorting and evaluating the slips.

Contrast this to the usual situation where each of several committees or task forces submits a report. Sifting through the prose, highlighting key ideas, and condensing information postpones feedback. And it takes the edge off creativity.

The slips become pawns, knights, and bishops in a chess game. Or think of them as cards in a game of solitaire. One physically manipulates ideas until a winning arrangement appears. The worth of an idea often depends on the company it keeps. This method stimulates the user to form new combinations. And at any stage, one can add new cards to the deck.

Professor Crawford compared his method to winding up a powerful spring. Each turn of the winding key stores up a little more energy. Each member of the group, by giving the problem one new twist, provides a tremendous store of energy. The problem solvers are ready to release that energy when they start manipulating the papers.

Spending a great amount of time on a problem doesn't guarantee high-quality solutions. Depth, thoroughness, systematic arrangement of ideas, and new combinations are the trump cards. Slip writing makes all of these possible.

How to Make Slip Writing Work

The leader should prepare for the slip-writing session by walking the whole process through in his mind several times. Explanations should be rehearsed and then edited for brevity and clarity.

Although any facet of a problem or opportunity works for slip writing, "how can we. . ." questions yield the highest returns on a first effort. Specificity is golden. "How can we help company engineers prepare better articles for our company magazine?" will give a better payoff than, "How can we improve the engineering section of our magazine?"

If a specific question is impossible, don't hesitate to use something more general. A first "general question" round of slip writing can produce the specific subquestions for later sessions.

Have the question printed and distributed on "trigger sheets" before the meeting. This gives the participants time to reflect, discuss, and incubate ideas. If slip writing is to be conducted as part of a dinner meeting, a trigger sheet can be located at each place setting. If trigger sheets are impossible, a poster, projection, or other aid can make the question visible.

Plan the tools and logistics. Provide each person with about 25 slips of three-by-five inch paper. Have extra pencils ready and plan a method for collecting the slips. Boxes or other containers placed at strategic points can serve as "idea banks."

The explanation should be no longer than five minutes. It should tell the group that they are going to participate in a new type of problem solving that will produce 50 to 100 (or more) new ideas. Then, introduce the question and explain its importance. The participants should attempt to get a flow of ideas going. Each idea should be written on a separate slip. They should not pause to evaluate the ideas or to write supporting rationales. Thoughts such as, "We tried that already," or "This may be illegal" should be put aside. Tell the participants who will process the ideas and how they can get an edited list if they want one.

Once the slips are collected, the leader or leadership team is ready to play solitaire. The slips should be sorted into various categories, related ideas together. Then, they can be evaluated and regrouped, using categories such as usefulness, impact, originality, and cost.

Extending the Method

Crawford slip writing need not be limited to "how to" questions. Any stage of a decision-making activity can use the method to advantage.

Identifying Problems

One manager holds periodic "clouds on the horizon" sessions. He asks his subordinates to anticipate problems that may appear six months to a year in advance. The anonymity of slip writing is ideally suited for such forecasting. It allows the subordinates to express insecurities about the operation. It relieves anxieties, upgrades problem awareness, and prompts both problem prevention and contingency planning.

Also, slip writing helps a manager get a grip on all the strings that make up an especially knotty problem. Each component of the problem is recorded on a separate slip. Sorting the slips helps the manager lay out relationships and locate the strategic issue.

Fact Finding

A decision and commitment to action should grow out of a thorough familiarity with up-to-date statistics, research, and forecasts. Here, slip writing can answer two questions:

- What facts do we need before we make a decision?
- How can we get accurate information quickly?

Evaluating a Decision

All of the slip-writing applications so far have used the suspension of judgment principle. A "murder board" breaks that rule. Here, slip writing helps exterminate all the bugs in a project before it is launched. The manager places before the group a marketing plan, a folder, or a sales approach. Each bug, that is, each statement of what someone dislikes, is written on a separate slip.

A murder board helps to prevent embarrassing and costly oversights. And it gives critics of a plan a chance to voice reservations that might otherwise ferment into dissention. Warning: These sessions are painful to the fathers of the item being pounded; it is vital that they leave the room before criticism starts.

Other Applications

Professor Crawford suggested that a management team apply slip writing over a period of several days prior to a meeting. Each member of the team is given a question and told to spend 15 minutes a day writing slips. The slips are spread out on the conference table during the meeting, and the manipulation of ideas becomes a team effort.

Who says questions and answers should come *after* a speaker makes a presentation? Collect questions before the speaker talks and give him a chance to read through the slips before the speech. This improves communication. It primes listener awareness, and it helps the speaker direct his comments to that particular audience.

Group slip writing can be varied by asking participants to count off in twos, then pair with a partner. One serves as recorder by writing slips for himself and the partner.

The slips also give instructors in training courses a quick way to improve teaching. The slips can be used after a briefing, a film, or a class. Ask each person to write all of the things that he or she liked about the presentation, then all of the things disliked. Allow 45 seconds at the end for participants to put plus signs on the positive slips and minus signs on the negative slips. The feedback is invaluable. It is immediate, and it saves the chore of sifting through bundles of reaction sheets.

STORMING FOR IDEAS

Persons who brainstorm regularly are repeatedly amazed at how the technique stimulates an explosion of ideas, along with strong surges of positive feeling. It's something like the process that takes place inside a nuclear pile. Neutrons bump into atoms and detach more neutrons. The process escalates, wrenching more particles out of their orbits and releasing huge amounts of energy. In brainstorming, ideas are allowed to hit each other in random order. The collisions bump other ideas out of their ruts or stereotypical contexts, releasing more energy and more idea-particles. And round it goes, until it's a hurricane of thought.

Brainstorming had the misfortune of starting on Madison Avenue. Critics had a field day making remarks about "group-think," "creativity by committee," and "cerebral popcorn"—noisy efforts with little nutritional value.

In the first 15 years after Alex Osborn of BBDO introduced the idea, over 75 American corporations asked for staff members to be trained in brainstorming. Corning Glass used it to find new uses for glass in automobiles; General Electric used brainstorming in value engineering; BFGoodrich made it a part of work simplification; and Westinghouse—as well as other firms—include brainstorming as an essential tool in their quality circles. IBM became a brainstorm booster, as did Union Carbide, Armstrong Cork, and 3M.

Brainstorming created and spread a climate favorable to new ideas. More than that, it has a track record for creating billions of dollars in cost-saving and profit-making concepts.

Much has been learned about brainstorming since the 1950s. Used on the wrong problems or with the wrong persons, it fails miserably. Without the right preparation, brainstorming sessions are disasters. Without proper follow-up, hundreds of newly created brainchildren end up imprisoned in a filing cabinet.

Brainstorming is, indeed, an unstructured process for generating ideas. But success requires that certain work be carried on before the session, during the session, and after the session.

Consider, for example, Allied Chemical Corporation's efforts to reduce energy consumption. Initiated by the director of energy resources, the program began with an extensive analysis of the company's 24 main industrial processes. From these, senior management selected five key processes: those that consumed the most energy or that seemed to offer the greatest promise for reduction of energy consumption. Teams of six to ten engineers participated in preliminary brainstorming sessions, one for each of the processes. After the meeting, they incorporated their most promising ideas into a 40-page briefing document that presented a step-by-step profile of the process, along with other vital technical information.

This set the stage for the key brainstorming sessions. Eight to 12 of the company's most knowledgeable technical experts—chemists, directors of technical centers, plant superintendents, and technical supervisors—were invited to brainstorm. Participants received a briefing document in advance of the meeting.

After each session, the leaders categorized the ideas according to technical feasibility, expense of implementation, and need for additional research. The first category alone (ideas that were technically feasible and capable of immediate implementation) promised as much as an 11 percent reduction in energy consumption for each process.

The program succeeded because it used brainstorming within the framework of good business planning, established clear objectives, and set priorities. Technical analysis became a partner in the creative action, and participants came to the sessions primed for creative output. Finally, the program established the machinery for speedy evaluation, reporting, and implementation.

Certainly, brainstorming preparation need not be this extensive and elaborate. But the planning principles still apply.

Before Brainstorming

Select a specific problem or opportunity and emphasize action through a "how to" phrasing. General questions, such as, "How can we improve company communications?" do not work well. The ideas scatter into so many divisions and categories that no density emerges for any one area. A more specific statement, such as, "How can we improve communications between our regional offices and world headquarters?" is vastly superior. In the case of Allied Chemical, the question came down to something as specific as, "How can we reduce energy consumption in our toluene diisocyanate process?"

Brief participants in advance on the problem and its background. A short document—even a one-page statement—may be sufficient. This starts a person's subconscious mind whirling so that the meeting can begin in high gear. Send a written invitation nailing down the time and place for the session.

There is no magic number for how many persons to invite. Groups of six to 12 work well. With groups larger than 12, there is a tendency for too many persons to talk at once. Break larger groups into teams of five or six persons each. Each team tackles the problem in its own huddle.

It helps to mix men and women and to bring in persons from different backgrounds and varying degrees of experience with the problem. Inviting the best people for the problem at hand will give the best results. Sometimes, however, the experts are so closely involved with the problem that they overlook fresh alternatives. Often, a nontechnical person can give a new perspective to a technical problem.

Consider positions and personalities when composing the guest list. Usually ideas come more fluently if the boss or supervisor does not brainstorm with the people who report directly to him. Lower-level employees may feel intimidated in the presence of senior executives, or tempted to show off. The presence of one piece of brass tempts participants to become brass polishers.

Experiment with different methods of recording ideas. Waiting for the secretary to catch up slows down the flow and interaction of suggestions. A tape recorder is unobtrusive, but writing ideas on a large piece of newsprint spurs new combinations. Several recording techniques can be used simultaneously.

Develop tactics to stimulate a spontaneous flow of ideas, drawing from the suggestions in the section that follows.

During Brainstorming

Often, a manager opens a meeting by saying, "Here's the problem. Let's have some suggestions." This is not brainstorming.

The rapid-fire, freewheeling flow and random collision of ideas trigger the creative explosion of a brainstorm. The context must be open and free from idea obstacles. The leader should know how to refuel a group if the heat dies down.

A statement of the problem, written in the "how to" form, should be posted in clear view. The leader can give a brief introduction to the problem—no more than three to five minutes.

The participants should read through the four rules of brainstorming. These can be posted or distributed on printed sheets.

1. Criticism of an idea—any idea—must be withheld until the session is over. Nothing kills creative thinking more than the person who says, "Oh—that will never work."
2. "Free wheeling" is not only permitted, but also encouraged. The more unusual the idea the better. It is much easier to build on an idea than to come up with an idea in the first place.

3. Quantity, as well as quality, is wanted. The greater the number of ideas, the greater our chances of getting some good ones.
4. "Hitch-hiking" is wanted. In addition to contributing ideas of his or her own, each member of the group should think of ways in which the suggestions of others can be built into better ideas, or how two or more ideas can be combined into a still better idea.

The leader may wish to review the rules by asking each person, in turn, to read one rule aloud and explain its meaning in different words. This helps the group grasp the rules. And it makes each person at ease with the sound of his or her own voice.

Some groups are more prone to using killer phrases than others. The leader must support the suspension of judgment principle at all costs. But he or she should not add insult to injury by criticizing a participant for criticizing. Anticipating the problem, the leader can use one of several tactics for repressing idea stoppers.

One technique is to give a few examples of killer phraes, then use Crawford slip writing to collect typical killers used in the corporation. Reading the phrases aloud drives the point home and loosens up the group.

The use of "red lights" and "green lights"—circles cut from construction paper—can keep judgment suspended during the brainstorming. Each participant receives one red light and one green light. The green light is up during the flow of positive ideas. Should someone let a killer phrase (or some other form of disapproval) slip out, the others can flag him to a stop.

Used with sensitivity, other techniques can incite idea flow and interaction during the session.

- The leader may wish to reproduce the S-C-A-M-P-E-R acronym from page 16 on a poster or projection. Reference to those principles stimulates more activity: "Which of the ideas mentioned so far can be combined?" "Can any be magnified or miniaturized?"
- Ask the person recording to read back every third idea. Pause after each to allow new associations to come forth.
- Ask selected individuals to pick an idea from the list and say something positive about it.

- Add an idea of your own—something you've been saving for the purpose.

Intense brainstorming can exhaust a group in 30 to 45 minutes. Set a time limit. If ideas are still spurting out at the end of the period, extend the session for another three to five minutes. Or say, "We have 65 ideas. Let's try for 75." Always quit while you are ahead. Never push a new group to the point of fatigue.

After Brainstorming

Send each of the brainstorming participants a complete list of ideas gathered during the session—as soon as possible. But no one can make sense out of a random list. Arrange the ideas into related groups before they are reproduced.

Participant feedback can spearhead implementation. Along with the idea list, send a covering memo that asks each person to (1) review the list and select the idea or combination of ideas that seem most promising, (2) add four or five suggestions about how to put the idea into action, and (3) return the idea and action suggestions by a specified date.

The leader may be tempted to ask for feedback on more than one idea. But a concentrated response on one is more valuable than good intentions—and vague notions—on six. The participants should feel free, of course, to act on other good ideas that fall within the scope of their jobs.

5

Matrix Charting

THE distance chart on the back of a service station map is the simplest form of matrix. A list of cities runs across the top, with the same list down the side. The boxes show the mileage between any two points. As a creative tool, the matrix chart uses "ideas" or "elements of a problem" in place of cities. Unlike the service station map, the ideas or elements that run across the top are usually different from those along the side.

Matrix charting will never replace the lengthy incubation period needed for individual genius. But it does stimulate the mind to see new connections and unexpected relationships. Often, there is a transformation of viewpoint, as if one were seeing the entire landscape for the first time. The chart can make associations happen. One is no longer at the mercy of the subconscious mind, which often takes too long a time to boil over.

The matrix chart is the newest tool in the creativity tool collection. This chapter represents a pioneer explanation of some of its creative uses. The possibilities are unlimited. It's like that day when the coach first passed out fiberglass poles to his pole vaulters. Who knows how high one of them will soar until the tool is tried out?

Persons who "teach creativity" soon become aware of how extreme responses to a new idea can be. On the one hand, a manager looks at the seed of an idea and says, "What's this speck of dust doing on my desk? What significance does this have for me?" Another manager, responding to the same seed, will say, "Now *this* has possibilities. Have you showed it to Bob Brown yet?" The idea triggers off a flow of responses. It's exciting to watch the person's mind work.

The first reaction is like crossing two dead electrical wires. The contact is there, but nothing happens. No sparks fly, no current flows. What tools are needed to help such persons make a connection?

That question led to considerable experimentation with matrix charts, until the simplest format—that presented on page 48—emerged as the leading answer.

This matrix does nothing more than systematize the questions creative persons naturally ask when they first meet up with a new idea. Often, they're not even aware that they're asking the questions.

First, use the matrix along with your personal reading. Skim through a newspaper or magazine such as *Business Week, Fortune, Chemical and Engineering News,* or *Rubber and Plastics News* until a new idea pops up. Write the idea at the top of one of the columns, then ask all the questions. Write answers in the appropriate squares. If no answer is immediately apparent, go on to the next question.

In ingenuity seminars, participants team up and interview each other with the questions to force more answers into the open. But there's no reason why the matrix won't work when used alone or with a colleague.

The tool can help all employees in a department or division become idea scouts for the firm. Consider how many tools a corporation supplies its members to help with mental work: pencils, executive desk sets, calculators, clocks, professional publications, and so forth. Think about the investments firms make to send employees to "idea cafeterias": management training courses, professional meetings, and conventions.

Tools such as the matrix chart—along with education on how to use them—multiply return on such investments by adding idea scouts to the payroll. What kind of improvement would a company make if it had 20 percent more idea people on the prowl?

Firms take it for granted that they will supply employees with the proper tools for doing mental work. For competitive reasons, they try to keep up with the state of the art. Some firms will make a

"There are solutions looking for problems as well as problems looking for solutions."

Insert New Ideas Here ⟶

Sources Include:
- Reading   ● Recreation
- Shopping   ● Colleagues

What else can I do with that?				
Where else can I use it?				
Who else can use it?				
When else can I use it?				
How else can I use it?				
Why else can I use it? (What other purposes are there?)				

breakthrough by supplying their employees with idea tool kits and guidance in how to use them.

DEVELOPING THE MATRIX

Matrices evolve. Often, the chart maker needs to switch elements—interchange the items that run across the top with those along the side—until one arrangement or the other feels right. Developing a matrix means playing with parts: dependent and independent variables, basic components, actions and reactions. As yet, no universal generalizations on how to set up a matrix have emerged. But the chart maker knows when he or she has hit on the right arrangement and combination. Ideas tumble out of every box.

Take, for example, the food processing industry's superb reputation for marketing new idea combinations: vitamin cereal, freeze-dried coffee, toaster waffles, pancake suppers, milkshake breakfasts, and summer soups.[3] Each product emerges through the unexpected combination of two words. Some pairs, such as toaster waffles, strike an agreement between product and method of preparation. Others, such as freeze-dried coffee, link process and product. The milk shake breakfast invites an old product to a new meal.

Any combination of categories—product against package, product with appliance used for preparation, product with process—can be explored on a matrix.

In a search for new package-product opportunities, someone might begin with an inventory of current package ideas from a trip to the local supermarket, plus some reading in the trade magazines. The various kinds of cans, boxes, and bags could be listed across the top of the matrix. The food products under consideration would go down the side.

The matrix user begins by X-ing out those combinations, such as boxed cereal and cans of coffee, that do not merit further exploration. Each of the other intersections invites reflection. Some unlikely combinations will surface: aerosol jelly, for example, or a cocktail on a stick. But such startling improbabilities may

[3]For more extensive treatment of this idea, see Edward M. Tauber, "HIT: Heuristic Ideation Technique—A Systematic Procedure for New Product Search," *Journal of Marketing*, Vol. 36 (January, 1972), pp. 58-70.

well suggest something that *does* work. The matrix user finds himself wondering why no one ever hit on that particular combination before.

Think of other uses. Charting established products and new products against established and potential markets can help the marketing department plot a channel through the most promising intersections. In strategic planning, anticipated environmental changes can be plotted against planning components. The matrix clarifies how one action will link up with and impact elements in the environment.

MATRIX FOR GROUP COMMUNICATIONS

Anyone who shoulders the responsibility for group presentations—meetings, sales briefings, staff training programs—faces the basic problem of how to keep the audience awake. Most persons, including those who make the presentations, are fed up with sit-and-listen meetings. They know that *telling* doesn't ensure communications, yet they pour out their ideas in the manner of a college lecturer. The point is this:

- Most meeting planners seek variety and impact in their ways to present stimuli.
- Too often, no attention is given to how audience reactions can be used to maximize responses.
- As a result, we end up with one-way communication, even though the communication effort is an expensive, ten-projector media event.
- The leaders complain about apathy and poor motivation.

The problem is this: the leaders spend a great effort on how to stimulate the audience, but direct no planning toward the audience response. The government, business, and voluntary sectors will continue their horrendous waste of brainpower and creative energy until they find ways of planning responses as part of their communication strategy.

Two basic elements—stimulus and response—suggest the framework for this matrix chart. The stimuli run down the side, and the audience reactions go across the top.

This matrix gives the group leader a tool for planning both

Matrix for Planning Powerful Meetings

STIMULI / REACTIONS	Listening	Watching	Asking Questions	Slip Writing	Pair Dialogues	Buzz Groups	And More . . .
Talks							
Exhibits							
Charts							
Overhead transparancies							
Slides							
Movies							
And more . . .							

materials and audience reaction. Working simultaneously with ideas, media, and responses, he or she can plot a sequence, rhythm, and climax for the meeting. Each medium can be linked up with one or more responses. Action is built into the meeting.

A more extensive list of matrix applications will someday merit a book in itself. It mobilizes the creative mind in any situation where relationships matter.

6

Starting an Idea Corps in Your Company

PRESCRIPTIONS for creativity should, in all honesty, carry proper warning labels. Reading about creativity often stirs up a mounting desire to try the creative experience. First, consider the costs as well as the benefits of creativity. To go back to the pole vaulting analogy for a moment: the new tools promise some truly exciting possibilities. But a person should look at the strains and hazards of the sport before leaping.

THE COSTS OF CREATIVITY

Creative persons face new frustrations because of increased problem awareness. And the more persons become sensitive to problems, the more despair they let themselves in for. They are struck by the full complexity of the issues, as well as the full scope of their new responsibilities.

Creative persons face new frustrations because of increased opportunity awareness. For example, they see new opportunities to advance their careers or to expand the firm's business. But often no one in authority seems willing to release the time or resources to mine the gold that is there. Others will say that the opportunities aren't gold ore, but hunks of rock. Then comes the pain of seeing a competitor or a colleague profit by digging at the same site.

Creativity adds up to a lot of hard work. Many individuals feel overscheduled already. Their appointment calendars are full. Often, however, they have become overly busy with the 80 percent of the work that—if done perfectly—accounts for only 20 percent of the results. They keep busy to avoid the pain, frustration, and worry of tackling the important work, the 20 percent that matters. Reweighing priorities is hard work. Implementing ideas is even harder.

Creativity adds new risks to life. This means new tensions, new anxieties. Some executives crave creativity/innovation, yet they don't want any change. This is a contradiction. Creativity implies something new, nonconforming, or different. And change means trouble.

Also, the more confidence a person builds with the creativity tools, the more pioneering that person becomes. He or she will be taking the initiative, knowing full well *who is accountable* if the idea fails.

An idea can fail. There are no panaceas for solving problems creatively or magic potions for imaginative opportunity finding. A first try may be a disaster. Or it may be below the standards set by others, and most certainly below the standards creative individuals set for themselves.

THE BENEFITS OF CREATIVITY

Note that the costs have to do with feelings of uneasiness and pain. In like manner, the rewards have to do with the feelings of joy and satisfaction.

A person gets the thrill of making breakthroughs. There's a joy in cracking a tough problem. In a very personal way, everyone has "eureka" experiences, where the heart leaps up because of a sudden discovery. These moments are memorable. No matter how many years ago an event happened, one remembers vividly the joy of coming up with a creative solution.

Persons get the thrill of building something bigger than themselves. Men and women like to feel they make a difference, that their contributions count. It's satisfying to see one's own ideas at work. Those ideas have contributed to the department, the company, and perhaps to the world. All persons have deep cravings to be part of a team that is doing something worthwhile.

A person gets the satisfaction of making new friendships. This comes partly because creative persons are more interesting themselves. He or she becomes more than a customer or spectator in the organization. The doers in an organization are few, and they usually welcome assistance.

Creative persons increase their chances for financial reward. Skill in creativity increases personal worth. With success comes the courage and confidence to take on more valuable problems and opportunities.

STARTING AN IDEA CORPS

Here are several suggestions for actions a person can take to stimulate creative thinking in his or her organization.

Start in a no-risk way with an idea buddy. Two persons can use slips; two persons can brainstorm or work with matrix charts. Two can share information about exhibits in the idea museum and prod each other out of ruts.

Some individuals experiment with the creativity tools at home with their families on such questions as, "How can we have the best vacation we've ever had?" or "How can we have more family fun on weekends?" Others try them out with one or two persons at work. Still others explore their possibilities in clubs or other organizations.

Start any program at work in a small way; let success ripple outward. Creativity is caught as well as taught. If a leader starts using creativity tools to produce results, one can be sure that the word will spread. Experiment with small projects before launching a departmental or companywide campaign.

Learn more about creativity techniques. The tools presented in this briefing are only a small part of the complete tool kit. Creativity seminars work, but be sure the instructor is creative himself and that he has a track record with businessmen. When a new management practice becomes popular, everyone begins to offer seminars. Anyone with platform presence and the ability to read three more books than his class can set up shop. People buy this thin broth, tasty to be sure, and then wonder why there's no nourishment in it.

Do some reading. Any librarian can help with this. Some firms have regular computer searches made to turn up articles on new

55

developments in the creativity/innovation field. Write for the free, nine-page catalog of materials available from:

The Creative Education Foundation
1300 Elmwood Avenue
Buffalo, N. Y. 14222

Investigate programs that use different combinations of creativity tools along with other special techniques. These include quality circles, job enrichment programs, value engineering, and work simplification. The idea corps starts with one or two leaders who are willing to become familiar with ways to enhance individual and group creativity and then find ways of diffusing those ideas to colleagues.